Mastering Cybersecurity Testing Tools: A Comprehensive Guide

ASHOK REDDY

DEDICATION

To the developers and contributors of Nmap, Burp Suite, Metasploit, Wireshark, and OWASP ZAP, whose innovation and dedication have made this book possible.

To my mentors and colleagues in the cybersecurity community, for your invaluable insights and unwavering support.

To my family and friends, for your endless patience and encouragement throughout this journey.

And to all cybersecurity professionals and enthusiasts, may this book empower and inspire you to make our digital world safer.

CONTENTS

ACKNOWLEDGEMENT

Creating "Mastering Cybersecurity Testing Tools: A Comprehensive Guide" has been an enlightening journey, and I am deeply grateful to those who have supported me along the way.

I extend my sincere gratitude to the developers and contributors of Nmap, Burp Suite, Metasploit, Wireshark, and OWASP ZAP. Your innovative work has been the backbone of this book.

A heartfelt thanks to my mentors and colleagues in the cybersecurity community. Your insights, feedback, and encouragement have been invaluable. Special thanks to those who reviewed drafts and provided critical guidance.

I am grateful to the organizations and institutions that champion cybersecurity education. Your resources and support have been instrumental.

Thank you to my publisher and the editorial team for your unwavering support and professionalism throughout this process.

To my family and friends, your patience and encouragement have been a constant source of strength.

Finally, to my readers, thank you for choosing this book. I hope it serves as a valuable resource in your cybersecurity journey.

Thank you all.

CHAPTER 1: INTRODUCTION TO CYBER-SECURITY TESTING

In today's digital age, cybersecurity is of paramount importance. With the ever-increasing complexity and sophistication of cyber threats, organizations must be vigilant in safeguarding their digital assets against potential attacks. Cybersecurity testing plays a crucial role in this endeavor, providing a systematic approach to identifying and mitigating vulnerabilities in information systems. In this chapter, we will explore the fundamentals of cybersecurity testing, its importance in maintaining robust security posture, and the various techniques and methodologies used in the process.

1.1 Understanding Cybersecurity Testing

Cybersecurity testing, also known as security testing or ethical hacking, is the process of evaluating the security of an organization's digital infrastructure by identifying vulnerabilities, weaknesses, and potential entry points for cyber attacks. It involves a systematic examination of networks, systems, applications, and other digital assets to assess their susceptibility to security breaches and unauthorized access. Cybersecurity testing is conducted using a variety of techniques, tools, and methodologies, with the ultimate goal of identifying and remediating security risks before they can be exploited by malicious actors.

1.2 Importance of Cybersecurity Testing

In today's interconnected world, where organizations rely heavily on digital technologies to conduct business, cybersecurity testing is more critical than ever. The consequences of a successful cyber attack can be severe, ranging from financial losses and reputational damage to legal liabilities and regulatory penalties. By proactively identifying and addressing security vulnerabilities, cybersecurity testing helps organizations mitigate these risks and safeguard their digital assets against potential threats. Furthermore, cybersecurity testing is essential for ensuring compliance with industry regulations and standards, such as the Payment Card Industry Data Security

Standard (PCI DSS) and the Health Insurance Portability and Accountability Act (HIPAA), which mandate regular security assessments and audits.

1.3 Objectives of Cybersecurity Testing

The primary objectives of cybersecurity testing can be summarized as follows:

➤ **Identifying Vulnerabilities:** Cybersecurity testing aims to uncover security vulnerabilities and weaknesses within an organization's digital infrastructure, including networks, systems, applications, and databases.

➤ **Assessing Security Controls:** Cybersecurity testing evaluates the effectiveness of existing security controls and measures, such as firewalls, intrusion detection systems (IDS), and antivirus software, in protecting against cyber threats.

➤ **Testing Incident Response Plans:** Cybersecurity testing assesses an organization's incident response capabilities by simulating cyber attacks and evaluating the effectiveness of response procedures and protocols.

➤ **Measuring Security Posture:** Cybersecurity testing provides insights into an organization's overall security posture, enabling stakeholders to identify areas of improvement and allocate resources more effectively to mitigate security risks.

➤ **Ensuring Compliance:** Cybersecurity testing helps organizations ensure compliance with industry regulations, standards, and best practices, thereby reducing the risk of legal liabilities and regulatory penalties.

1.4 Types of Cybersecurity Testing

Cybersecurity testing can be classified into several distinct types, each serving a specific purpose and providing valuable insights into different aspects of an organization's security posture. Some of the most common types of cybersecurity testing include:

> **Vulnerability Assessment:** Vulnerability assessment involves identifying and prioritizing security vulnerabilities within an organization's digital infrastructure, including networks, systems, and applications. This type of testing helps organizations identify weaknesses that could be exploited by cyber attackers and prioritize remediation efforts based on the severity of the vulnerabilities.

> **Penetration Testing:** Penetration testing, also known as pen testing or ethical hacking, involves simulating cyber attacks against an organization's digital infrastructure to identify and exploit security vulnerabilities. Penetration testers, often referred to as ethical hackers, use a variety of techniques and tools to probe networks, systems, and applications for weaknesses and potential entry points for cyber attacks.

> **Security Auditing:** Security auditing involves evaluating an organization's security controls and measures to ensure compliance with industry regulations, standards, and best practices. Security auditors assess the effectiveness of existing security controls, identify areas of improvement, and provide recommendations for enhancing the organization's overall security posture.

> **Incident Response Testing:** Incident response testing involves simulating cyber attacks and evaluating an organization's incident response capabilities. This type of testing helps organizations assess the effectiveness of their incident response procedures and protocols, identify gaps and weaknesses in their response capabilities, and improve their overall readiness to respond to cyber security incidents.

> **Red Team Exercises:** Red team exercises involve simulating sophisticated cyber attacks against an organization's digital infrastructure to test its defenses and response capabilities. Red teams, often composed of experienced security professionals, use advanced techniques and tools to mimic the tactics, techniques, and procedures (TTPs) of real-world cyber attackers, providing valuable insights into an

organization's security posture and readiness to defend against advanced threats.

1.5 Key Principles of Cybersecurity Testing

Several key principles guide the practice of cybersecurity testing and ensure its effectiveness in identifying and mitigating security risks:

> **Risk-Based Approach:** Cybersecurity testing should be conducted based on an organization's specific risk profile, taking into account its industry, size, complexity, and regulatory requirements. By focusing on the most critical assets and highest-priority risks, organizations can maximize the impact of cybersecurity testing and allocate resources more effectively.

> **Comprehensive Coverage:** Cybersecurity testing should encompass all aspects of an organization's digital infrastructure, including networks, systems, applications, databases, and cloud environments. By conducting comprehensive assessments, organizations can identify and address security vulnerabilities across the entire attack surface.

> **Continuous Monitoring:** Cybersecurity testing should be conducted on a regular and ongoing basis to ensure that security vulnerabilities are promptly identified and remediated. By adopting a proactive approach to security testing, organizations can stay ahead of emerging threats and minimize the risk of security breaches.

> **Collaborative Approach:** Cybersecurity testing should involve collaboration and communication among various stakeholders, including IT teams, security teams, management, and third-party vendors. By fostering collaboration and sharing information, organizations can improve their security posture and respond more effectively to cyber threats.

> **Adaptive Strategy:** Cybersecurity testing should be flexible

and adaptive, evolving in response to changes in the threat landscape, technology, and business environment. By continuously evaluating and refining their testing strategies, organizations can stay ahead of emerging threats and maintain a strong security posture.

1.6 Conclusion

In conclusion, cybersecurity testing is a critical component of any comprehensive cybersecurity program, enabling organizations to identify and mitigate security vulnerabilities before they can be exploited by cyber attackers. By adopting a risk-based approach, conducting comprehensive assessments, and continuously monitoring their security posture, organizations can enhance their resilience to cyber threats and protect their digital assets against potential attacks. In the subsequent chapters of this book, we will delve deeper into the various techniques, tools, and methodologies used in cybersecurity testing, providing readers with practical insights and guidance on how to effectively assess and enhance the security posture of their organizations.

Chapter 2: Nmap (Network Mapper)

Nmap, short for Network Mapper, is a powerful and versatile open-source tool designed for network discovery and security auditing. Developed by Gordon Lyon, commonly known as Fyodor, Nmap has become a staple in the arsenal of cybersecurity professionals, network administrators, and ethical hackers worldwide. In this chapter, we will explore Nmap in depth, covering its history, features, installation, basic usage, advanced techniques, scripting capabilities, and real-world applications.

2.1 History of Nmap

Nmap traces its origins back to the late 1990s when Fyodor began developing the tool as a hobby project while studying computer science at the University of Illinois. Initially released in 1997, Nmap quickly gained popularity within the cybersecurity community for its ability to provide comprehensive network reconnaissance and security auditing capabilities. Over the years, Nmap has undergone numerous updates and enhancements, evolving into a mature and feature-rich tool that remains at the forefront of network scanning and security assessment.

2.2 Features of Nmap

Nmap offers a wide range of features and functionalities, making it a versatile tool for network discovery, mapping, and security auditing. Some of the key features of Nmap include:

- ➤ **Host Discovery:** Nmap can identify hosts that are active on a network, even those configured to evade detection by traditional means such as ICMP ping requests.

- ➤ **Port Scanning:** Nmap can scan for open ports on target systems, providing insights into potential entry points for cyber attackers and services running on those ports.

- ➤ **Service Version Detection:** Nmap can determine the version of services running on open ports, aiding in vulnerability assessment and exploit targeting.

➢ **Operating System Detection:** By analyzing subtle differences in network responses, Nmap can accurately infer the operating system running on a target machine, providing valuable insights into the composition of a network environment.

➢ **Scriptable Interaction:** Nmap's scripting engine allows users to automate and customize their scans, extending its functionality to suit specific requirements and scenarios.

2.3 Installation of Nmap

Installing Nmap is a straightforward process, as it is available for a wide range of operating systems, including Windows, Linux, macOS, and others. Depending on the operating system, users can choose from various installation methods, such as package managers, precompiled binaries, or source code compilation. Detailed installation instructions for each operating system can be found on the official Nmap website (https://nmap.org/).

2.4 Basic Usage of Nmap

Getting started with Nmap involves mastering its basic usage commands, which allow users to perform a variety of network reconnaissance and security auditing tasks. Some of the most commonly used commands include:

➢ **Scanning a Single Host:** Use the command nmap [IP address or host name] to scan a specific host and identify open ports.

➢ **Scanning a Range of IP Addresses**: Specify a range of IP addresses using nmap [first IP]-[last IP] to scan multiple hosts simultaneously.

➢ **Scanning a Subnet:** Utilize the subnet mask to scan an entire network segment with nmap [subnet mask].

➢ **Performing OS Detection:** Add the -O flag to enable OS detection capabilities, revealing the operating system of target hosts.

➢ **Performing Service Version Detection:** Use the -sV flag to instruct Nmap to probe for service versions running on open ports.

These basic usage commands serve as the foundation for conducting network scans and security assessments using Nmap.

2.5 Advanced Techniques with Nmap

While Nmap's basic usage commands provide a solid foundation for network scanning and security auditing, the tool also offers a plethora of advanced techniques and options for more sophisticated assessments. Some of the advanced techniques and options include:

➢ **Timing Options:** Nmap allows users to adjust the timing of scans to balance between speed and stealth, with options ranging from aggressive scans to stealthy scans that minimize detection.

➢ **Output Formats:** Nmap supports various output formats, including plain text, XML, and grepable formats, allowing users to customize the output to suit their preferences and analysis tools.

➢ **Host Discovery Techniques:** In addition to traditional ping-based host discovery, Nmap offers alternative host discovery techniques, such as ARP scanning, TCP ACK scanning, and reverse-DNS resolution.

➢ **Service and Version Detection Scripts:** Nmap's scripting engine, known as NSE (Nmap Scripting Engine), provides a vast collection of scripts for performing specialized tasks, such as detecting specific services and versions, identifying vulnerabilities, and conducting brute-force attacks.

➢ **Firewall Evasion Techniques:** Nmap includes techniques for evading firewall restrictions and network filters, such as fragmented packet scanning, idle scanning, and decoy scanning.

Mastering these advanced techniques and options allows users to conduct more nuanced and effective network scans and security assessments using Nmap.

2.6 Scripting Capabilities of Nmap

One of the most powerful features of Nmap is its scripting engine, NSE (Nmap Scripting Engine), which allows users to extend the functionality of the tool through custom scripts. Nmap scripts are written in the Lua programming language and can be used to automate repetitive tasks, perform complex analysis, and customize scan behavior. Some common uses of Nmap scripts include:

➢ **Vulnerability Detection:** Nmap scripts can detect and exploit common vulnerabilities in target systems, such as misconfigured services, outdated software, and weak authentication mechanisms.

➢ **Service Enumeration:** Nmap scripts can enumerate services running on target systems, providing detailed information about their configuration, version, and potential security risks.

➢ **Brute-Force Attacks:** Nmap scripts can conduct brute-force attacks against authentication mechanisms, such as SSH, FTP, and Telnet, to test the strength of passwords and credentials.

➢ **Information Gathering:** Nmap scripts can gather additional information about target systems, such as network topology, routing information, and open ports, to aid in reconnaissance and analysis.

2.7 Real-World Applications of Nmap

Nmap finds widespread application in various cybersecurity scenarios, ranging from network reconnaissance and vulnerability assessment to penetration testing and incident response. Some common real-world applications of Nmap include:

- ➤ **Network Discovery:** Nmap is commonly used by network administrators to discover and map networked devices, identify rogue devices, and assess the overall health and security of the network infrastructure.

- ➤ **Vulnerability Assessment:** Security professionals use Nmap to conduct vulnerability assessments of target systems, identifying potential security vulnerabilities, misconfigurations, and weaknesses that could be exploited by attackers.

- ➤ **Penetration Testing:** Ethical hackers and penetration testers use Nmap to simulate cyber attacks against target systems, identifying entry points, exploiting vulnerabilities, and demonstrating the potential impact of real-world attacks.

- ➤ **Incident Response:** During incident response investigations, security teams use Nmap to gather forensic evidence, assess the scope and impact of security incidents, and identify compromised systems and services.

2.8 Conclusion

In conclusion, Nmap is a versatile and powerful tool for network discovery, mapping, and security auditing. With its extensive feature set, flexible configuration options, and scripting capabilities, Nmap provides cybersecurity professionals, network administrators, and ethical hackers with the tools they need to conduct comprehensive assessments of networked systems and infrastructure. By mastering the basics of Nmap, exploring its advanced techniques and options, and leveraging its scripting capabilities, users can enhance their ability to identify and mitigate security risks, safeguarding against potential cyber threats and attacks.

Chapter 3: Metasploit Framework

3.1 Introduction to Metasploit Framework

The Metasploit Framework is an advanced open-source penetration testing platform that enables security professionals, ethical hackers, and penetration testers to assess and exploit vulnerabilities in target systems. Developed by Rapid7, Metasploit provides a comprehensive suite of tools, modules, and payloads for conducting penetration tests, exploiting security vulnerabilities, and simulating cyber attacks. In this chapter, we will explore the history, features, architecture, and components of the Metasploit Framework, as well as its role in modern cybersecurity testing.

3.2 History of Metasploit Framework

The history of the Metasploit Framework dates back to 2003 when it was initially created by H.D. Moore as an open-source project aimed at developing a comprehensive platform for exploiting security vulnerabilities. Over the years, Metasploit has evolved into one of the most widely used penetration testing frameworks in the cybersecurity industry, with contributions from a vibrant community of developers, researchers, and security professionals. Today, Metasploit remains at the forefront of offensive security research and penetration testing, driving innovation and advancement in the field of cybersecurity.

3.3 Features of Metasploit Framework

Metasploit offers a wide range of features and functionalities that make it a versatile and powerful tool for penetration testing and vulnerability assessment. Some of the key features of the Metasploit Framework include:

➢ **Exploit Development:** Metasploit provides a platform for developing, testing, and deploying custom exploits for security vulnerabilities in target systems.

➤ **Payload Generation:** Metasploit offers a variety of payloads, including shellcode, reverse shells, and meterpreter, for executing arbitrary commands on compromised systems.

➤ **Post-Exploitation Modules:** Metasploit includes a collection of post-exploitation modules for conducting various activities on compromised systems, such as privilege escalation, lateral movement, and data exfiltration.

➤ **Exploit Database:** Metasploit integrates with the Exploit Database (EDB), a comprehensive repository of exploits and vulnerability data, providing access to a vast collection of exploits for testing and research purposes.

➤ **Automation and Scripting:** Metasploit supports automation and scripting through its command-line interface (CLI) and scripting language, allowing users to streamline penetration testing workflows and customize their testing procedures.

3.4 Architecture of Metasploit Framework

The Metasploit Framework is designed around a modular architecture that consists of several components working together to facilitate penetration testing and vulnerability assessment. The main components of the Metasploit Framework architecture include:

➤ **Console:** The Metasploit console provides an interactive command-line interface (CLI) for interacting with the framework, executing commands, and managing penetration testing tasks.

➤ **Modules:** Metasploit modules are the building blocks of the framework and include exploits, payloads, auxiliary modules, and post-exploitation modules for conducting various tasks during penetration tests.

➤ **Exploit Modules:** Exploit modules in Metasploit contain code that exploits security vulnerabilities in target systems to gain unauthorized access or execute arbitrary commands.

➢ **Payload Modules:** Payload modules in Metasploit generate and deliver payloads to compromised systems, allowing attackers to execute commands, establish remote connections, and interact with compromised hosts.

➢ **Auxiliary Modules:** Auxiliary modules in Metasploit perform additional tasks during penetration tests, such as port scanning, fingerprinting, and vulnerability scanning.

➢ **Post-Exploitation Modules:** Post-exploitation modules in Metasploit enable attackers to maintain persistence, escalate privileges, and extract sensitive information from compromised systems after successful exploitation.

3.5 Installation and Configuration of Metasploit Framework

Installing and configuring the Metasploit Framework is a relatively straightforward process, as it is available as an open-source project with precompiled binaries and installation scripts for various operating systems. Depending on the target platform, users can choose from different installation methods, such as package managers, manual installation from source code, or prebuilt virtual machine images. Additionally, Metasploit provides options for customizing the framework's configuration settings, such as network parameters, logging options, and module preferences, to suit specific penetration testing requirements.

3.6 Basic Usage of Metasploit Framework

Getting started with the Metasploit Framework involves mastering its basic usage commands and workflows, which allow users to conduct penetration tests, exploit security vulnerabilities, and simulate cyber attacks effectively. Some of the most commonly used commands and workflows in Metasploit include:

➢ **Starting the Metasploit Console:** Launching the Metasploit console and connecting to the framework's backend services.

➢ **Loading Modules:** Loading exploit, payload, auxiliary, and post-exploitation modules into the Metasploit console.

➢ **Searching for Modules:** Searching the Metasploit module database for specific exploits, payloads, or auxiliary modules.

➢ **Configuring Modules:** Configuring module options, such as target IP addresses, ports, and payloads, before running exploits or auxiliary tasks.

➢ **Running Exploits:** Executing exploit modules against target systems to exploit security vulnerabilities and gain unauthorized access.

➢ **Generating Payloads:** Generating payloads using payload modules and delivering them to compromised systems to establish remote connections or execute commands.

➢ **Post-Exploitation Tasks:** Running post-exploitation modules on compromised systems to maintain persistence, escalate privileges, and extract sensitive information.

3.7 Advanced Techniques with Metasploit Framework

In addition to its basic usage commands and workflows, the Metasploit Framework offers a wide range of advanced techniques and options for conducting more sophisticated penetration tests and security assessments. Some of the advanced techniques and options available in Metasploit include:

➢ **Advanced Exploit Development:** Developing custom exploits for zero-day vulnerabilities and proprietary software applications.

➢ **Exploit Suggester:** Using the Exploit Suggester module to automatically identify potential exploits for target systems based on installed software versions and known vulnerabilities.

➢ **Meterpreter Shell:** Leveraging the Meterpreter shell, a powerful post-exploitation tool, for executing commands, pivoting through networks, and interacting with compromised systems.

➢ **Payload Encoding:** Encoding payloads to evade antivirus detection and bypass security controls during penetration tests.

➢ **Exploit-DB Integration:** Integrating Metasploit with the Exploit Database (EDB) to access the latest exploits and vulnerability data for testing and research purposes.

3.8 Scripting Capabilities of Metasploit Framework

One of the most powerful features of the Metasploit Framework is its scripting capabilities, which allow users to automate penetration testing tasks, customize exploit workflows, and extend the functionality of the framework through custom scripts. Metasploit scripting is based on the Ruby programming language and provides access to a wide range of APIs, libraries, and utilities for interacting with the framework's components and modules. Some common use cases for Metasploit scripting include:

➢ **Automating Penetration Tests:** Writing scripts to automate repetitive penetration testing tasks, such as scanning for vulnerabilities, exploiting security flaws, and extracting sensitive information from target systems.

➢ **Customizing Exploit Workflows:** Developing custom exploit workflows and attack chains tailored to specific target environments, applications, or security configurations.

➢ **Extending Framework Functionality:** Creating custom modules, payloads, and post-exploitation tasks to extend the functionality of the Metasploit Framework and address unique penetration testing requirements.

3.9 Real-World Applications of Metasploit Framework

The Metasploit Framework finds widespread application in various cybersecurity scenarios, ranging from penetration testing and vulnerability assessment to red teaming and adversary simulation. Some common real-world applications of Metasploit include:

➢ **Penetration Testing:** Using Metasploit to identify and exploit security vulnerabilities in target systems, applications, and networks during penetration tests and security assessments.

➢ **Vulnerability Assessment**: Leveraging Metasploit's exploit modules, auxiliary tasks, and post-exploitation capabilities to assess the security posture of organizations and prioritize remediation efforts based on identified vulnerabilities.

➢ **Red Teaming:** Employing Metasploit as part of red teaming exercises to simulate sophisticated cyber attacks, test defensive capabilities, and evaluate incident response procedures in realistic scenarios.

➢ **Adversary Simulation:** Using Metasploit to mimic the tactics, techniques, and procedures (TTPs) of real-world cyber adversaries and assess an organization's readiness to defend against advanced threats and targeted attacks.

3.10 Conclusion

In conclusion, the Metasploit Framework is a powerful and versatile penetration testing platform that provides security professionals, ethical hackers, and penetration testers with the tools they need to assess and exploit vulnerabilities in target systems effectively. With its comprehensive suite of features, modular architecture, scripting capabilities, and real-world applications,

Metasploit remains an indispensable tool for offensive security research, vulnerability assessment, and red teaming exercises. By mastering the fundamentals of Metasploit, exploring its advanced techniques and options, and leveraging its scripting capabilities, users can enhance their ability to conduct comprehensive penetration tests, identify security weaknesses, and improve the overall security posture of organizations.

CHAPTER 4: WIRESHARK

4.1 Introduction to Wireshark

Wireshark is a powerful and versatile open-source network protocol analyzer that allows users to capture, analyze, and interpret network traffic in real-time. Developed by the Wireshark development team, Wireshark provides a comprehensive suite of tools and features for network troubleshooting, protocol analysis, security monitoring, and forensic investigations. In this chapter, we will explore the history, features, architecture, and components of Wireshark, as well as its role in modern cybersecurity testing and network analysis.

4.2 History of Wireshark

The history of Wireshark traces back to the late 1990s when it was initially developed as an open-source project called Ethereal by Gerald Combs. Originally released in 1998, Ethereal quickly gained popularity within the networking and security communities for its ability to capture and analyze network packets in real-time. In 2006, the project was renamed Wireshark due to trademark issues, and development continued under the new name. Since then, Wireshark has evolved into one of the most widely used network protocol analyzers in the world, with contributions from a global community of developers, researchers, and enthusiasts.

4.3 Features of Wireshark

Wireshark offers a wide range of features and functionalities that make it a versatile and powerful tool for network analysis and troubleshooting. Some of the key features of Wireshark include:

➢ Packet Capture: Wireshark can capture network packets in real-time from various network interfaces, including Ethernet, Wi-Fi, and Bluetooth.

➢ Protocol Decoding: Wireshark can decode and dissect a wide range of network protocols, including TCP/IP, UDP, HTTP, DNS, and SSL/TLS, providing detailed insights into network traffic.

➢ Filters and Display Options: Wireshark allows users to apply filters and display options to focus on specific packets, protocols, conversations, or endpoints, making it easier to analyze complex network traffic.

➢ Packet Analysis: Wireshark provides tools for analyzing packet headers, payloads, and metadata, as well as identifying errors, anomalies, and security threats in network traffic.

➢ Protocol Statistics: Wireshark generates statistics and summaries for different network protocols, such as packet counts, byte counts, retransmission rates, and round-trip times, facilitating performance monitoring and troubleshooting.

4.4 Architecture of Wireshark

Wireshark is designed around a modular architecture that consists of several components working together to capture, analyze, and interpret network traffic. The main components of the Wireshark architecture include:

➢ Capture Engine: The capture engine in Wireshark is responsible for capturing network packets from various sources, such as network interfaces, pcap files, and remote capture devices.

➤ Packet Dissection Engine: The packet dissection engine in Wireshark is responsible for decoding and dissecting network packets, extracting protocol headers, payloads, and metadata, and presenting the information in a human-readable format.

➤ Display Filter Engine: The display filter engine in Wireshark is responsible for applying filters and display options to network packets, allowing users to focus on specific packets, protocols, conversations, or endpoints during analysis.

➤ Protocol Support: Wireshark supports a wide range of network protocols out-of-the-box, including TCP/IP, UDP, HTTP, DNS, SSL/TLS, SSH, and SMB, as well as custom and proprietary protocols through protocol dissectors and plugins.

4.5 Installation and Configuration of Wireshark

Installing and configuring Wireshark is a relatively straightforward process, as it is available as an open-source project with precompiled binaries and installation packages for various operating systems. Depending on the target platform, users can choose from different installation methods, such as package managers, standalone installers, or source code compilation. Additionally, Wireshark provides options for customizing the application's configuration settings, such as capture options, display preferences, and protocol dissectors, to suit specific network analysis requirements.

4.6 Basic Usage of Wireshark

Getting started with Wireshark involves mastering its basic usage commands and workflows, which allow users to capture, analyze, and interpret network traffic effectively. Some of the most commonly used commands and workflows in Wireshark include:

➢ Starting a Capture: Initiating a packet capture session in Wireshark to capture network packets in real-time from various network interfaces.

➢ Filtering Packets: Applying display filters and display options to focus on specific packets, protocols, conversations, or endpoints during analysis.

➢ Analyzing Packets: Examining packet headers, payloads, and metadata, as well as identifying errors, anomalies, and security threats in network traffic.

➢ Protocol Statistics: Generating statistics and summaries for different network protocols, such as packet counts, byte counts, retransmission rates, and round-trip times, for performance monitoring and troubleshooting.

➢ Exporting Data: Exporting captured packets, analysis results, and protocol statistics to external files, such as pcap files, CSV files, or plain text files, for further analysis or reporting purposes.

4.7 Advanced Techniques with Wireshark

In addition to its basic usage commands and workflows, Wireshark offers a wide range of advanced techniques and options for conducting more sophisticated network analysis and troubleshooting tasks. Some of the advanced techniques and options available in Wireshark include:

➢ Packet Reconstruction: Reassembling fragmented packets, decoding encrypted traffic, and reconstructing application-layer protocols, such as HTTP, FTP, and SMTP, for in-depth analysis.

➤ Flow Analysis: Analyzing network flows, sessions, and conversations to identify patterns, trends, and anomalies in network traffic, such as network congestion, bandwidth usage, and protocol violations.

➤ Expert Analysis: Using Wireshark's built-in expert system to automatically detect and flag potential issues, errors, and security threats in network traffic, such as malformed packets, protocol violations, and suspicious activity.

➤ Protocol Dissectors: Writing custom protocol dissectors and plugins to support custom and proprietary protocols, extend Wireshark's protocol support, and enhance its network analysis capabilities.

➤ Command-Line Interface: Leveraging Wireshark's command-line interface (CLI) and scripting capabilities to automate network analysis tasks, customize analysis workflows, and integrate Wireshark with other tools and frameworks.

4.8 Real-World Applications of Wireshark

Wireshark finds widespread application in various cybersecurity scenarios, ranging from network troubleshooting and performance monitoring to intrusion detection and forensic investigations. Some common real-world applications of Wireshark include:

➤ Network Troubleshooting: Using Wireshark to diagnose and troubleshoot network connectivity issues, performance bottlenecks, and application errors in real-time.

➤ Protocol Analysis: Analyzing network protocols, application-layer traffic, and communication patterns to identify vulnerabilities, misconfigurations, and security risks in networked systems.

➤ Intrusion Detection: Deploying Wireshark as part of an intrusion detection system (IDS) to monitor network traffic for suspicious activity, unauthorized access attempts, and potential security breaches.

➢ Forensic Investigations: Using Wireshark to collect, analyze, and interpret network traffic as part of forensic investigations into cyber attacks, data breaches, and other security incidents.

4.9 Conclusion

In conclusion, Wireshark is a powerful and versatile network protocol analyzer that provides security professionals, network administrators, and IT professionals with the tools they need to capture, analyze, and interpret network traffic effectively. With its comprehensive suite of features, modular architecture, and real-time analysis capabilities, Wireshark remains an indispensable tool for network troubleshooting, protocol analysis, security monitoring, and forensic investigations. By mastering the fundamentals of Wireshark, exploring its advanced techniques and options, and leveraging its scripting capabilities, users can enhance their ability to analyze and interpret network traffic, identify security vulnerabilities, and mitigate potential risks effectively.

CHAPTER 5: BURF SUITE

5.1 Introduction to Burp Suite

Overview: Burp Suite is a widely used web application security testing tool developed by PortSwigger. It helps security professionals perform comprehensive security assessments of web applications, identifying vulnerabilities and potential attack vectors.

Importance in Web Application Security: In an era where web applications are integral to business operations, securing them against cyber threats is crucial. Burp Suite provides a robust platform for detecting security flaws, ensuring applications are resilient against attacks.

Capabilities and Limitations:

➢ **Capabilities:**

- o Interception and modification of HTTP/S traffic.
- o Automated scanning for vulnerabilities.
- o Advanced manual testing capabilities.
- o Extensible via custom scripts and plugins.

➢ **Limitations:**

- o Primarily focused on web applications.
- o Requires expertise to use effectively for advanced testing.
- o May not handle some non-standard or heavily obfuscated protocols well.

5.2 History of Burp Suite

Origins and Founders: Burp Suite was created by Dafydd Stuttard, also known as PortSwigger, in the early 2000s. The tool emerged from a need for a flexible and powerful web application security testing platform.

Evolution Over the Years:

> **Early Days:** Initially a simple proxy tool, it allowed basic interception and analysis of HTTP traffic.

> **Growth and Expansion:** Over the years, features like automated scanning, the Intruder for attack automation, and more advanced tools such as the Repeater and Sequencer were added.

> **Major Milestones:** Significant updates include the introduction of the Burp Suite Professional version with advanced capabilities, Burp Suite Enterprise for continuous security testing, and numerous community-developed plugins.

Impact on the Security Industry: Burp Suite has become a cornerstone tool for web application security professionals. Its comprehensive feature set and user-friendly interface have made it a go-to for both automated and manual testing, significantly contributing to the advancement of web application security practices.

5.3 Key Features of Burp Suite

Interceptor: The Interceptor tool allows users to intercept, inspect, and modify HTTP and HTTPS traffic between their browser and the target application. This is the foundation for manual web application testing.

> **Usage:**

- o Set up the browser to use Burp Suite as a proxy.
- o Intercept requests and responses in real-time.
- o Modify parameters to test for vulnerabilities such as SQL injection, XSS, and others.

Scanner: Burp Suite's Scanner is an automated tool that identifies security vulnerabilities in web applications. It uses various techniques to discover issues such as cross-site scripting (XSS), SQL injection, and insecure direct object references.

- ➢ **Configuration:**

  - o Launch a scan against a target application.
  - o Customize scan configurations for different testing needs.
  - o Analyze the scan results to identify and prioritize vulnerabilities.

Intruder: Intruder is used to perform automated attacks on web applications to identify vulnerabilities.

- ➢ **Capabilities:**

  - o Fuzzing input fields to find common vulnerabilities.
  - o Brute forcing authentication mechanisms.
  - o Performing parameterized attacks using custom payloads.

Repeater: Repeater allows testers to manually modify and resend individual HTTP requests to see how the application responds.

- ➢ **Usage:**

  - o Send requests from the Proxy or Scanner to Repeater.
  - o Modify parameters and headers.
  - o Resend requests and analyze responses to pinpoint vulnerabilities.

Sequencer: Sequencer analyzes the quality of randomness in session tokens and other critical data items.

➤ **Configuration:**

- o Capture tokens or other items for analysis.
- o Evaluate their randomness and security implications.

Decoder and Comparer:

➤ **Decoder:** Convert data between different formats (e.g., URL-encoded, Base64).

➤ **Comparer:** Compare different items (e.g., responses) to identify differences and potential security issues.

Use Case Scenarios:

➤ **Intercepting Login Forms:** Modify and replay login requests to test authentication mechanisms.

➤ **Automated Vulnerability Scanning:** Run scans to identify common web application vulnerabilities.

➤ **Manual Testing with Repeater:** Test specific inputs and responses to uncover nuanced vulnerabilities.

➤ **Token Analysis with Sequencer:** Ensure session tokens are secure and unpredictable.

5.4 Architecture of Burp Suite

Core Components and Their Interactions:

➤ **Proxy:** Central to Burp Suite, it intercepts all HTTP/S traffic for inspection and modification.

➤ **Tools Integration:** Each tool (Scanner, Intruder, Repeater, etc.) works in tandem with the Proxy, sharing data and enabling comprehensive testing workflows.

> **Session Handling:** Manages sessions and cookies across different tools, ensuring a consistent testing environment.

Extension Mechanisms:

> **BApps Store:** A marketplace for Burp extensions that add new features and integrations.

> **Custom Extensions:** Users can write their own extensions using the Burp Extender API, supporting Java, Python, and Ruby.

Data Processing Workflow:

> **Traffic Interception:** Data flows from the browser through Burp Proxy.

> **Analysis and Modification:** Tools like Repeater, Intruder, and Scanner process this data, performing analysis and potential modifications.

> **Result Aggregation:** Results from various tools are aggregated for review and further action.

5.5 Installation and Configuration

System Requirements:

> **Operating Systems:** Compatible with Windows, macOS, and Linux.
> **Hardware:** Minimum of 4 GB RAM and dual-core CPU recommended for optimal performance.

Step-by-Step Installation Guide:

1. **Download Burp Suite:**
   o Visit the PortSwigger website and download the appropriate installer for your OS.
2. **Install the Software:**
   o Follow the installer instructions for your specific OS.
   o On Linux, you may need to set executable permissions using `chmod +x`.

Configuration for Optimal Use:

➢ **Proxy Setup:**
   o Configure your browser to use Burp Suite's proxy settings.
   o Install the Burp Suite CA certificate in the browser to intercept HTTPS traffic.

➢ **Scanner Settings:**
   o Customize scan settings to suit your testing scope and objectives.
   o Set the scan speed and depth based on the complexity of the target application.

➢ **User Options:**

   o Configure settings such as project files, request throttling, and automated backup to streamline your workflow.

5.6 Basic Usage of Burp Suite

User Interface Navigation:

➢ **Dashboard:** Overview of the current project, including active scans and recent activity.

➢ **Target Tab:** Define the scope of your testing and view site maps.

➢ **Proxy Tab:** Intercept, view, and modify HTTP/S traffic.

➢ **Intruder, Repeater, Scanner, and Sequencer Tabs:** Access to the specific tools for detailed analysis and testing.

Proxy Setup:

➢ **Interception:**
  o Set the Proxy to intercept traffic.
  o Use the Inspector to analyze and modify HTTP requests and responses.
➢ **HTTP History:**
  o Review captured traffic in the HTTP history tab.
  o Analyze request-response pairs to identify potential vulnerabilities.

Performing Basic Tasks:

➢ **Capturing Requests:**

  o Browse the target application with the proxy enabled.
  o Burp Suite captures and logs all HTTP/S requests and responses.

➢ **Modifying Responses:**

  o Intercept requests and modify parameters to test for vulnerabilities.
  o Replay modified requests and analyze server responses.

➢ **Analyzing Traffic:**

- o Use the various tabs (e.g., Site Map, HTTP History) to review captured data.
- o Identify anomalies or patterns that may indicate security issues.

5.7 Advanced Techniques with Burp Suite

Scanner Configuration for Advanced Users:

> **Custom Scan Profiles:**

- o Create tailored scan profiles for specific applications or testing scenarios.
- o Adjust settings such as crawl depth, audit speed, and issue definitions.

> **Handling Complex Workflows:**

- o Configure Burp to handle multi-step processes like login sequences or complex form submissions.

Advanced Intruder Setups:

> **Payload Positions:**

- o Select specific parts of the HTTP request to insert payloads.
- o Use positions to test various input fields and headers.

> **Payload Types:**

- o Utilize built-in payload sets or create custom payloads.

o Employ payload encoders and payload processors for more complex attacks.

> **Attack Types:**

o Sniper: Single payload at one position.
o Battering ram: Single payload across multiple positions.
o Pitchfork: Different payloads across multiple positions simultaneously.
o Cluster bomb: Combine multiple payloads in all possible combinations.

Scripting and Automation:

> **Burp API:**

o Use the Burp Extender API to automate tasks and extend Burp's functionality.
o Examples include automating repetitive testing tasks or integrating Burp with other tools.

> **Custom Extensions:**

o Write custom extensions in Java, Python (via Jython), or Ruby.
o Leverage community libraries and frameworks to enhance your scripts.

5.8 Real-World Applications of Burp Suite

Case Studies:

> **Case Study 1: E-commerce Website Security Testing:**
　o Identify common vulnerabilities in shopping carts, payment gateways, and user authentication mechanisms.

> **Case Study 2: Financial Application Penetration Testing:**

  o Ensure robust security for online banking systems, focusing on data integrity and user authentication.

Common Vulnerabilities Identified with Burp Suite:

> **Cross-Site Scripting (XSS):**
> > o Detecting and exploiting XSS vulnerabilities using automated and manual testing techniques.

> **SQL Injection:**
> > o Identifying SQL injection points and testing with payloads to exploit database access.

> **Broken Authentication and Session Management:**
> > o Testing for weak session tokens, poor password policies, and insecure login mechanisms.

> **Security Misconfiguration:**
> > o Identifying default settings, incomplete configurations, and exposed sensitive data.

Expert Insights:

> **Best Practices for Using Burp Suite:**
> > o Leverage insights from experienced security professionals on effective Burp Suite use.

> **Tips and Tricks:**
> > o Practical tips for optimizing workflow, managing large projects, and handling complex security tests.

5.9 Integrations and Extensibility

Integrating with Other Tools:

- ➤ **CI/CD Pipelines:**
  - o Integrate Burp Suite with continuous integration and continuous deployment (CI/CD) pipelines for automated security testing.

- ➤ **External Tools:**
  - o Use tools like JIRA for issue tracking, Jenkins for automation, and Splunk for logging and analytics.

- ➤ **APIs and Webhooks:**
  - o Set up integrations using APIs and webhooks to trigger actions and retrieve data.

Using BApps:

- ➤ **BApp Store:**
  - o Explore and install BApps from the Burp Suite App Store to extend Burp's capabilities.
  - o Examples of popular BApps include those for advanced scanning, reporting, and enhanced analysis.

- ➤ **Developing Your Own BApps:**
  - o Write custom BApps to tailor Burp Suite to specific needs.
  - o Share your BApps with the community or keep them private for internal use.

Community Contributions:

- ➤ **Notable Extensions:**
  - o Review and utilize community-developed extensions that enhance Burp Suite's functionality.
  - o Contributions from security experts worldwide offer valuable additions to your toolkit.

- ➤ **Resource Sharing:**

o Participate in community forums, share insights, and collaborate on projects to stay updated with the latest advancements.

5.10 Conclusion

Summary of Learning:

➢ Recap the key points covered in the chapter, highlighting Burp Suite's role in web application security testing.

➢ Emphasize the importance of both automated and manual testing in identifying and mitigating vulnerabilities.

The Future of Burp Suite:

➢ Speculate on future developments and updates from PortSwigger.

➢ Discuss emerging trends in web application security and how Burp Suite is expected to evolve to address new challenges.

Continuing Education and Resources:

➢ **Official Documentation and Tutorials:**
   o Refer readers to Burp Suite's official documentation and online tutorials for ongoing learning.

➢ **Books and Courses:**
   o Recommend books, online courses, and certifications that focus on advanced Burp Suite usage and web application security.

➢ **Community and Forums:**

o Encourage participation in security forums, webinars, and workshops to stay connected with the community and up-to-date with the latest practices.

Chapter 6: OWASP ZAP (Zed Attack Proxy)

6.1 Introduction to OWASP ZAP

Overview: OWASP ZAP (Zed Attack Proxy) is an open-source web application security scanner maintained by the Open Web Application Security Project (OWASP). It's designed to find security vulnerabilities in web applications during development and testing phases.

Importance in Web Application Security: OWASP ZAP is widely used for discovering security flaws in web applications, such as SQL injection, cross-site scripting (XSS), and other vulnerabilities listed in the OWASP Top Ten. Its easy-to-use interface and powerful automation capabilities make it a vital tool for security professionals and developers.

Capabilities and Limitations:

> **Capabilities:**

- o Automated and manual vulnerability scanning.
- o Support for a wide range of web application protocols.
- o Extensive scripting and automation options.
- o Integration with other tools and CI/CD pipelines.

> **Limitations:**

- o Limited to web application security testing.
- o May require advanced configuration for complex applications.
- o False positives and negatives that require manual verification.

6.2 History of OWASP ZAP

Origins and Founders: OWASP ZAP was initiated by Simon Bennetts in 2010. As part of the OWASP community, it benefits from contributions by security experts worldwide.

Evolution Over the Years:

➤ **Early Versions:** Discuss the initial release and early functionalities of ZAP.

➤ **Feature Enhancements:** Highlight major updates and new features, such as the introduction of the HUD (Heads-Up Display), API integration, and advanced scanning techniques.

➤ **Community Contributions:** Explore how the OWASP community has influenced ZAP's development through plugins, scripts, and feedback.

Impact on the Security Industry: OWASP ZAP has significantly impacted the security industry by making web application security testing accessible to a broader audience, including small businesses and independent developers.

6.3 Key Features of OWASP ZAP

Automated Scanning:

➤ **Functionality:** Explanation of ZAP's automated scanning capabilities, including spidering, active scanning, and passive scanning.

➤ **Configuration:** Step-by-step guide to configuring automated scans for different types of web applications.

➤ **Interpreting Results:** How to analyze scan results, prioritize findings, and implement fixes.

Manual Testing Tools:

➤ **Intercepting Proxy:** Using ZAP as a proxy to intercept and modify HTTP/S traffic between the browser and the web application.

➤ **Fuzzer:** Leveraging the fuzzer tool to test for input validation vulnerabilities by sending various payloads to input fields.

➤ **Forced Browsing:** Discovering hidden resources and directories using the Forced Browsing tool.

Advanced Scripting and Automation:

➤ **Scripting Languages:** Overview of supported scripting languages, including JavaScript, Python, and Groovy.

➤ **Custom Scripts:** Creating custom scripts to automate specific security tests or integrate ZAP with other tools.

➤ **API Integration:** Utilizing ZAP's REST API for automated testing within CI/CD pipelines.

Heads-Up Display (HUD):

➤ **Introduction:** Explanation of the HUD feature that integrates ZAP directly into the browser, providing real-time feedback and alerts.

➤ **Usage Scenarios:** Practical examples of how to use the HUD for interactive security testing during web application development.

Alert Management:

- ➢ **Alert Handling:** Understanding ZAP alerts, their severity levels, and how to manage them.

- ➢ **Reporting:** Generating detailed reports of scan results, including customizable templates and formats.

6.4 Architecture of OWASP ZAP

Core Components and Their Interactions:

- ➢ **Component Overview:** Explanation of ZAP's core components, including the proxy, spider, scanner, and database.

- ➢ **Data Flow:** Describe how data flows through ZAP, from capturing requests to analyzing responses.

Extension and Plugin Architecture:

- ➢ **Plugins:** Overview of available plugins and extensions that enhance ZAP's functionality.

- ➢ **Developing Plugins:** Guide on creating custom plugins to extend ZAP's capabilities.

Data Processing Workflow:

- ➢ **Traffic Interception:** Detailed process of intercepting and analyzing HTTP/S traffic.
- ➢ **Scan Workflow:** Steps involved in a typical scanning process, from initial spidering to vulnerability detection.

6.5 Installation and Configuration

System Requirements:

> **Supported Platforms:** List of supported operating systems (Windows, macOS, Linux).

> **Hardware Requirements:** Minimum and recommended hardware specifications for running ZAP efficiently.

Step-by-Step Installation Guide:

> **Windows Installation:** Detailed instructions for installing ZAP on Windows, including screenshots.

> **macOS Installation:** Step-by-step guide for macOS installation.

> **Linux Installation:** Instructions for installing ZAP on various Linux distributions, including handling dependencies and permissions.

Configuration for Optimal Use:

> **Initial Setup:** Basic setup steps, including configuring the proxy and setting up SSL/TLS certificates.

> **Advanced Configuration:** Customizing ZAP settings for specific testing scenarios, such as configuring session management and authentication handling.

6.6 Basic Usage of OWASP ZAP

User Interface Navigation:

> **Main Dashboard:** Overview of the main dashboard and its components, including the sites tree, alerts tab, and workspace.

> **Tabs and Panels:** Explanation of the various tabs and panels, such as the history tab, breakpoints tab, and request/response viewers.

Proxy Setup:

> **Browser Configuration:** Steps to configure a browser to use ZAP as a proxy for intercepting traffic.

> **SSL/TLS Configuration:** Setting up SSL/TLS certificates to intercept HTTPS traffic.

Performing Basic Tasks:

> **Spidering:** How to use the spider to discover all accessible resources on a web application.

> **Active Scanning:** Conducting active scans to identify vulnerabilities.

> **Passive Scanning:** Utilizing passive scanning to detect issues without sending additional requests.

6.7 Advanced Techniques with OWASP ZAP

Advanced Scanning Techniques:

> **Context Configuration:** Setting up contexts to define different parts of the web application and apply specific scan policies.

> **Session Management:** Configuring session management to handle authenticated scans effectively.

> **User Management:** Creating and managing users for testing role-based access controls.

Custom Scripts and Extensions:

> **Script Types:** Overview of different types of scripts, such as active rules, passive rules, and HTTP sender scripts.

> **Script Creation:** Step-by-step guide to creating custom scripts for specific testing needs.

> **Extension Development:** Instructions for developing custom extensions to enhance ZAP's capabilities.

Automation and Integration:

> **CI/CD Integration:** Integrating ZAP with continuous integration and continuous deployment (CI/CD) pipelines.

> **Automated Scans:** Setting up automated scans using ZAP's command-line interface and API.

6.8 Real-World Applications of OWASP ZAP

Web Application Security Testing:

> **Vulnerability Detection:** Using ZAP to detect common web application vulnerabilities, such as SQL injection, XSS, and CSRF.

> **Security Assessments:** Conducting comprehensive security assessments and generating detailed reports for clients.

Case Studies:

> ➤ **Case Study 1: E-Commerce Application:** Analyzing how ZAP was used to identify and mitigate security vulnerabilities in a large e-commerce application.
> ➤ **Case Study 2: Financial Services:** Exploring the use of ZAP in securing a financial services platform and ensuring compliance with regulatory requirements.

Expert Insights:

> ➤ **Best Practices:** Recommendations from security experts on effectively using ZAP for various testing scenarios.

> ➤ **Tips and Tricks:** Practical tips for optimizing ZAP performance, capturing relevant traffic, and interpreting complex results.

6.9 Integrations and Extensibility

Integration with Other Security Tools:

> ➤ **Tool Compatibility:** Exploring how ZAP integrates with other security tools, such as Burp Suite, Metasploit, and SIEM platforms.

> ➤ **Data Export:** Exporting scan results in various formats for further analysis or reporting.

API and Automation:

> ➤ **ZAP API:** Detailed guide on using ZAP's REST API for automation and integration.
> ➤ **Scripting Automation:** Automating repetitive tasks with custom scripts and scheduled scans.

Community Contributions:

➢ **ZAP Marketplace:** Overview of the ZAP Marketplace, where users can find and share plugins, scripts, and extensions.

➢ **Community Forums:** Engaging with the OWASP ZAP community for support, collaboration, and knowledge sharing.

6.10 Conclusion

Summary of Learning:

➢ Recap the key points covered in the chapter, highlighting ZAP's role in web application security testing.

➢ Emphasize the importance of regular security testing and proactive vulnerability management.

Future Trends in Web Security Testing:

- Speculate on future developments in web security testing tools and techniques.
- Discuss emerging trends such as AI-driven security testing, increased focus on API security, and the shift towards DevSecOps

********************AR********************

www.ingramcontent.com/pod-product-compliance
Lightning Source LLC
Chambersburg PA
CBHW072002210526
45479CB00003B/1037